fungus
skull
eye
wing

Also by Alfonso D'Aquino

Astro Labio

Hyalus

Naranja verde

Basilisco

Víbora breve

Luciérnagas

Briznas

Tanagra

piedra no piedra

Prosfisia

Also translated by Forrest Gander

Pinholes in the Night: Essential Poems from Latin America (with Raúl Zurita)

Panic Cure: Poems from Spain for the 21st Century

Watchword, poems by Pura López Colomé

Spectacle and Pigsty, poems by Kiwao Nomura (translated with Kyoko Yoshida)

My Floating Mother City by Kazuko Shiraishi (translated with Samuel Grolmes, Yumiko Tsumura, and Tomoyuki Endo)

Firefly Under the Tongue, Selected Poems of Coral Bracho

The Night, A Poem by Jaime Saenz (with Kent Johnson)

Another Kind of Tenderness by Xue Di (with Keith Waldrop, et. al.)

No Shelter: The Selected Poems of Pura López Colomé

Immanent Visitor: Selected Poems of Jaime Saenz (with Kent Johnson)

Connecting Lines: New Poetry from Mexico

Mouth to Mouth: Poems by 12 Contemporary Mexican Women

fungus
skull
eye
wing

selected
poems of
Alfonso
D'Aquino

translated by
Forrest Gander

COPPER CANYON PRESS

PORT TOWNSEND, WASHINGTON

Cover art: Lorena Cassady, *Tlaloc ballplayer,* photograph, Xalapa Museum

Copper Canyon Press is in residence at Fort Worden State Park in Port Townsend,
Washington, under the auspices of Centrum. Centrum is a gathering place for artists and
creative thinkers from around the world, students of all ages and backgrounds, and
audiences seeking extraordinary cultural enrichment.

LIBRARY OF CONGRESS CATALOGING-IN-PUBLICATION DATA

Aquino, Alfonso D'.

fungus skull eye wing : selected poems of Alfonso D'Aquino / Alfonso D'Aquino ;
translated by Forrest Gander.

pages cm

ISBN 978-1-55659-447-2 (pbk.)

I. Aquino, Alfonso D'—Translations into English. II. Gander, Forrest, 1956–
translator. III. Aquino, Alfonso D'. Poems. Selections. III. Aquino, Alfonso D'. Poems.
Selections. English. IV. Title.

PQ7298.1.Q56A2 2013
861'.64—dc23

2013036851

98765432 FIRST PRINTING

COPPER CANYON PRESS
Post Office Box 271
Port Townsend, Washington 98368

www.coppercanyonpress.org

Acknowledgments

Thanks to the editors of the following publications, in which these poems first appeared in English:

Connotation Press: An Online Artifact: "Black Bee" and "*Digitaria Exilis*"
Interim: "Spores" and "Citron's Bitterness"
Literal: "(green flourite)"
Poetry Northwest: "Networks"
Qarrtsiluni: "Vertical Fish / *graffiti*" and "Frond"
S/N: New World Poetics: "Its Verb's Forked Tongue" and "(d)"
Tongue: A Journal of Writing & Art: "The Wolf's Dream / *intaglio*"

Poems in Spanish originally appeared in:

Astro Labio: "Acanto: b / sombra," El sueño del lobo / *intaglio*," "Abeja negra," "Pez vertical / *graffiti*," "*Digitaria exilis*," "Zagreo," "Escrito en un grano de sal," "(*green fluorite*)," "a /red," and "Sinsabor del acitrón"
Deshoras (inédito): "13"
Hoja suelta: "Esporas" and "Fronda"
Nudo (inédito): "El résped de su verbo" and (d)
Vegetaciones (inédito): "Redes"

Contents

ix   *A Note on Alfonso D'Aquino*

Part I

5   Acanthus: b / shadow

9   Frond

11   Networks

19   The Wolf's Dream / *intaglio*

21   Black Bee

23   Vertical Fish / *graffiti*

27   13

31   Spores

35   *Digitaria exilis*

Part II

39   Zagreus

Part III

53   Written in a Grain of Salt

55   (green fluorite)

61   Acanthus: a /net

63   Citron's Bitterness

67   Its Verb's Forked Tongue

71   [Knot]

74   *A Note on the Translation*

75   *About the Translator*

A Note on Alfonso D'Aquino

ALFONSO D'AQUINO was raised by his grandmother in an old house attached to a colonial convent in Coyoacán, Mexico. Books were his best friends from an early age. Often solitary, he spent many afternoons at a small aquarium in the nearby town of San Ángel, fascinated then (as now) by the nonhuman world.

D'Aquino makes his living as an editor, is the author and editor of several books for children, and teaches a Poetry and Silence workshop that, over ten years, has become as renowned and influential as those Poetry as Magic sessions that Jack Spicer conducted at the start of the San Francisco Renaissance. But D'Aquino's poems are less like Spicer's than they are like Hart Crane's. In "Zagreus," the poem that composes the middle sequence of this collection, we encounter the kind of private erotics that characterize so many of the poems in Crane's *White Buildings*. In addition to both poets' recourse to feminine iambic couplets, Crane's "stone of lust," his "crocus lusters of the stars," his "signature of the incarnate word," and his many references to mirrors and to Dionysus (who is linked to Zagreus) reverberate profoundly throughout D'Aquino's work.

Where D'Aquino currently lives, on the outskirts of Cuernavaca, the vegetation is jungly and the electricity goes out for days at a time. There are stars and behind the stars, stars. Snakes are his talismanic animals, and he has names for the different lizards doing push-ups on hot volcanic rocks in his garden. He collects local plants and knows their medicinal uses.

Octavio Paz, who recognized D'Aquino's talent early on and championed his work, was his first editor and organized the publication of his first collected poems in *Naranja verde* (Green orange). At the age of twenty-two, he was awarded the prestigious Carlos Pellicer Poetry Prize. Despite the early acclaim, D'Aquino has stayed clear of the combative circles of poets who live, by and large, in Mexico City. For a long time, he has chosen the solitude, the land, the ceiba trees. It's his attentiveness to the music (including the silence) of his body within particular landscapes that most distinguishes his writing. The prosody of his poems is nuanced, the rhythms counterpointed. The greatest difficulty in translating his work is trying to find new arrangements for his orchestrations of sound.

His many published books include such titles as *Vibora breve* (Small viper), *Basilisco* (Basilisk), *Naranja verde* (Green orange), and *piedra no piedra* (lapis no lapis). Yet, apart from this selection, there are no books of D'Aquino's work available in English. There are, however, translations by Rebecca Seiferle in the notable anthology *Reversible Monuments: Contemporary Mexican Poetry,* and in literary magazines I've come across excellent translations by Roberto Tejada and by James Ryang.

One of D'Aquino's lifelong concerns is the world that takes place parallel to the human world and our attitude toward it. Often, the syntax of his poetry braids together strands of relationship, emphasizing the mutuality of perceptual experience—the intertwining of the seer and the seen. In this sense, even though his poems are more bodily in their orientation than those of other poets in Mexico, his work has an intensely spiritual quality. A subjective point of view is nourished and sustained by its surround—the rocks, vipers, trees, and stars. Before there was such a word as "eco-poetry," D'Aquino was writing poems registering the complex interdependency that draws us into dialogue with the world. Not "nature poetry" as topic and commentary, but poetry as exploration (both formal and thematic) of the relationships between nature and culture, body and feeling, language and perception.

Forrest Gander

fungus
skull
eye
wing

Part I

Acanto

b / sombra

No se mueve la estatua
sino su sombra
que a lo largo del día
se hace redonda

Va trazando una raya
entre las piedras
y sus dedos alargan
la línea ciega

Por la luz que desciende
sobre su espalda
ha dorado las ramas
rojiza pátina

Con la mano desnuda
flores y hiedras
va rozando la sombra
las hojas nuevas

En la piedra se enciende
inquieta llama
la tarde transparenta
carne soñada

Hace señas la mano
oscuros signos
en lo alto del muro
racimos ígneos

Acanthus

b / shadow

The statue doesn't
but its shadow shifts
throughout the day
making a circle

It traces its own way
across the stones
fingering forward
along a blind edge

The light slanting
over its shoulder
tints the branches
with a reddish patina

Its hand points out
flowers and ivy
and new leaves
graze on the shadow

Over stones a restless
flame quivers
the afternoon transparentizes
the dream of flesh

The hand beckons
making dark signs
against the high wall
igneous clusters

No se mueve la estatua
sino su sombra
que a lo largo del día
se vuelve otra

The statue doesn't
but its shadow shifts
throughout the day
and returns a stranger

Fronda

No tiene ninguna forma
la hoja en medio
de las hojas

Las hojas no son el aile
sino el aire
que lo copa

Y una copa cabe en otra
dentro de una
sola hoja

Movimiento de la fronda
que desvela
otra rosa

Y una en otra se transforma
como un cielo
entre dos hojas

Invisible rama loca
se retuerce
por sí sola

Si una hoja y otra hoja
siempre son
la misma hoja

Veo por dentro de las hojas
movimiento de una a otra
que las ronda...

Todo el árbol una hoja
que contiene todo el aile
y otra hoja...

Apariencia de la fronda
que se enreda con las ramas
de otras hojas...

Veo por dentro de las formas
en las venas de las copas
la otra rosa...

Y el filoma se transflora
en el tejido invisible
que desdobla...

El estilo y la corola
espirales que se tiñen
y se ahondan...

Desde la rama no vista
a la sombra de esta hoja
que cae rota...

Frond

It's formless
the leaf in the middle
of the leaves

From within the leaves I see
one brushing another
that keeps it company...

Leaves aren't the alder
but the air
in its sleeve

All the tree a leaf
that holds all the alder
and more leaves...

And trees drink each other in
from one of them
a singular leaf

And a frond emerges
tangled in the branches
among the leaves...

Gesticulation of the frond
disclosing
another flower

From within its patterns I see
in the shadowed bower
the other flower...

And each moves into the other
like a sky
between two leaves

And the phylum transfloresces
invisibly woven and
opening out...

Wild invisible branch
twisting
into one form

The stalk and the corolla
spirals darkening
and digging in...

If one leaf and another leaf
always are
the same leaf

From the unseen branch
to the shade of this leaf
falling broken...

Redes

formas huecas
entrenudos entrevistos entre sueños
círculos   zacates   juncos

pálida albura tierna tiembla
semilla   baya   hierba

la percepción de cada brizna
la diferenciación de cada brizna
y los huecos que entre todas ellas brillan

cultivos de palabras
"las mil cosas que crecen"

tejido uniforme verde / *cambiantes figuras rosas*
líneas ocultas bajo tierra ocurren
y abren su espacio interno blando y nuevo
a medida que avanzan
y prolongan en la página oscura
hilos de tinta incandescente y blanca
la luz mueve los tallos
hojas   espinas   astros

veloz e interminable
escritura violeta entre las piedras
rasgos que absorben vidrios líquidos
labios absortos en los líquenes
líneas vivificadas
agraz ala limón agrafia
letras mudas

caligrafía de pelos absorbentes que dicen y desdicen
entre las partículas térreas que los cubren

Networks

resonant forms
internodes gleaned between dreams
cattails   grasses   circles

pale sapwood trembling tender
seed   berry   grass

the apperception of each blade
the distinction of each blade
and gaps gleaming between them all

crops of words
"the thousand growing things"

uniformly green weave / *shifting pink figures*
there are subterranean lines
that breach an internal latitude fresh and mellow
even as they push forward
across the dark page
inky threads incandescent and white
the light incites the stems
leaves   spines   stars

quickly and without end
a violet writing in the stones
marks limned with liquid glass
lips lured by lichens
enlivened lines
agrestal lemons drooping agraphia
and mute letters

a calligraphy of absorbent hairs saying and unsaying
in the earthy particulate that surrounds it

azufre   carbon   hierro
venas bajo las piedras refulgen

flexible precisión de las figuras
ni un movimiento de más
inaccesibles formaciones de las nubes
de las piedras   de la hierba
nervaduras   vistas   oscuras

qué dicen raíces
figuras huecas bajo tierra ocupan
figuras huecas llenas de tierra
lugares vacíos en los que nada falta

agua negra   granos   sales
que alimentan con sus ínfimas substancias
el esqueleto vítreo de la hierba

pecíolo   círculo   hueso
ápice   sépalo   centro

los tallos buscan la luz
las hojas duermen
con espontánea sutileza
la plántula despierta

verdeante entre musgos
semilla latente busco
lo que el ojo ya no ve
una vez deshechos o desdichos los nudos
que lo ataban al aire

una luz por sí sola salida no sé de dónde
paisajes nocturnos con briznas iluminadas
hierbas sin carne ni color / *su sola luz en el aire*

sulfur   carbon   iron
underveins in the rocks glitter

a ductile precision to the figures
and not an unnecessary move
inaccessible formations of clouds
of stones   of grass
a nervure   sensed   obscurely

the roots say what
hollow figures conquering an underground
hollow figures packed with dirt
empty places lacking nothing

black water   grain   salts
feeding with their tiny substances
the vitreous skeleton of grass

petiole   circle   bone
apex   sepal   center

stems seeking the light
leaves asleep
with spontaneous subtlety
the wakened shoot

bright green among the mosses
a dormant seed seeking
what the eye can't see
coming undone or unsaying themselves the knots
that bind seed to air

a singular light escaping from I don't know where
nocturnal landscapes with luminous blades
fleshless colorless grasses / *lifting their own light*

drupas   zumos   aromas
amentos   tépalos   violas

huecas figuras fulguran
en las formas entrevistas en los huecos de la fronda
aire donde nace un aile

orden secreto de las hierbas
movimiento   color   paso del viento

bajo mi piel de planta
bajo mi cara de animal
bajo mis huesos de piedra
bajo mi carne que es tierra
dentro de esta red de sal a ras cubierto
con el mantillo redivivo del que nazco
disociado de todos mis compuestos
húmedo hebroso verdezco

albo bulbo transluce
su carne transparente y lúcida

y en el reverso de las hojas veo
la radiante transparencia de su sombra
haces de partículas azules / *transparencia de las cosas*
y a contraluz los hilos que las cruzan
y me cruzan   y te cruzan
y otros en unos se tornan

sobre una hoja de papel en la que se refleja un vidrio
hoja de vidrio en que leo
la transparencia de la materia / *el paisaje disuelto*
alterno   momentáneo   sin texto

y en esta luz que en su caída incontenible
traspasa las piedras
bajo estratos invisibles y figuras vacías

drupes   juices   aromas
cattails   tepals   violets

hollow gleaming figures
in forms interseen through gaps in foliage
air giving birth to alders

secret order of the grasses
gesture   color   passage of wind

below my plant skin
below my animal face
below my stone bones
below my flesh which is earth
within this covering net of salt flush
with the revivifying mulch from which I'm born
decoupled from all my compounds
humid fibrous greening

an albid translucent bulb
its flesh transparent and lucid

and in the netherside of leaves I see
radiant transparence of their shadows
made of deckled blues / *the transparency of things*
embossed with crisscrossing threads
that pass through me   and through you
and others in turn

over a sheet of paper on which a window's light reflects
panes of glass through which I leaf
transparency of the particular / *the dissolved landscape*
no temporary   alternative   text

so in this light that on its stopless fall
pierces stones
under invisible strata and empty figures

la visión del abismo
radical quemadura preexistente
inextinguible más allá de sí mismo

impalpables   invisibles   indudables
hilos   rutilos   neutrinos

la visión del núcleo en cada nudo
en este prado circular
en torno a un árbol que ya no está

follaje espejo bajo el azul pensante
el rumor de las hojas
la multiplicación de los gestos
las historias entre la hierba
y el reflejo de la luna en cada una de las briznas
en sus oscilaciones profundas
llenan las ramas de sombras en movimiento

desencarnación del verbo
en el seno de la tierra
visto desde otro ángulo
una áspera luz encierra

interferencia   mezcla   oscilación
agua   cero   luz   cero   a   cero
los 11 mil ojos de la hierba viendo el sol

el secreto perdido entre la hierba
es la huella del verso bajo las estrellas

descenso al árbol de sombra que crece bajo su sombra
transparencia de los ailes bajo el oblicuo sol de la tarde
disolución de la madera en la luz de la luz en la materia

piedra desenterrada
hongo   cráneo   ojo   ala

a vision of the abyss
its radical preexistent blaze
beyond itself inextinguishable

impalpable   invisible   indubitable
rutilant   threads   neutrinos

a vision of the nucleus in each knot
in this circular meadow
around a tree that no longer exists

specular foliage under the thinking blueness
the rustle of leaves
the multiplication of gestures
stories coursing through grass
and the moon's reflection in all the blades
in their profound oscillations
hang moving shadows on the branches

so the unfleshing of the verb
in the earth's very lap
viewed at another angle
stroked by bitter light

oscillation   stirred into   interference
water   zero   light   zero   to   zero
the 11 thousand eyes of the grass fixed on the sun

a secret lost in the grass
goes to verse under turning stars

down the length of the tree shadow sprouts below shadow
transparence of awn below an afternoon's slanted sun
the wood dissolving in the light in light of the matter

unearthed stone
fungus   skull   eye   wing

El sueño del lobo / *intaglio*

Conciliábulo de grajos
en torno a un trozo de carne

Soñaba el lobo / que unos pájaros negros
desgarraban su piel a picotazos / —*y era cierto*

Uno iba en círculo / le rozaba los belfos
luego volaba a un árbol / y cantaba en silencio

Otro se afana en vano / con las patas abiertas
en arrancar del suelo / los restos de la presa

Grajo verdinegro / por mirar el cielo
parado en un tronco / tornasola el cuello

Mientras el lobo duerme / y aquel grajo regresa
la blancura se tiñe / el pájaro se atreve

Levanta con el pico / un ojo abierto y negro
y sacude las alas / y lo esconde en el suelo

Su sueño huele a sangre / los párpados entierra
si tan sólo lo inquieta / el canto de unas aves

Grajo verdinegro / cabeza de cuervo
un pájaro en otro / tornasola el viento

The Wolf's Dream / *intaglio*

Cabal of grackles
swarming a piece of meat

The wolf dreamed / several black birds
pierced its skin with their beaks /—*and it was true*

One circled / grazing the wolf's jowls
and landed in a tree / to caw in silence

Another plugs away / with splayed legs
at what remains of a carcass / in the dirt

Green-black grackle / eyeing the sky
standing on a stump / its neck iridescing

The grackle returns / while the wolf sleeps
its white fur ruddied / and the bird emboldened

Plucks up with its bill / an open black eye
and shaking its wings / plants the eye in the ground

The wolf's dream reeks of blood / buried eyelids
and the bother / of so many bird calls

Green-black grackle / raven's head
one bird in another / iridescing the wind

Abeja negra

Silabas
que
zumban
rezuman

dentro
de
mi
cabeza

miel
oscura

luces
son
horas

ecos
son
oros

agua
miel
latía
al
fondo
del
agua
viva

Silencio
espejo
silencio
hueco

irradia
en
la
arena
filamento
ardiente

solar
e
intrasolar
trasluz

del
ojo
al
objeto
viene

del
objeto
al
oro
va

Rezumbancia
magnética
del
hondo
laberinto
de
la
oreja

retorno
a
la
primera
y
única
colmena

interno
silencio
intenso

prístina
espina
dorada
que
se
adelgaza
en
el
agua

Silencio
hueso

su
resplandor
irrumpe
en
mi
cerebro

enjambre
espejo

donde
toda
la
noche
vi

imaginaria
y
africanizada

una
abeja
de
tierra
sutil

Black Bee

Syllables
that
buzz
ooze

inside
of
my
head

dark
honey

lights
are
hours

echo
as
gold

honey
water
beating
to the
bottom
of the
wakened
water

Silence
mirror
silence
recess

radiant
in
the
sand
filament
on fire

solar
and
intrasolar
driftlight

from the
eye
to the
coming
thing

from the
thing
to the
going
gold

Magnetic
zoom
of the
deep
labyrinth
of
the
ear

returning
to
the
first
and
only
hive

inmost
silence
intense

pristine
golden
thorn
thin-
ning
out
in
the
water

Bone
silence

its
splendor
erupting
in
my
brain

mirror
swarm

where
I saw
all
the
night

imaginary
and
Africanized

from
soft
dirt
a
bee

Pez vertical / *grafitti*

trazado con un dedo en la superficie salitrosa de un muro

con la vejiga llena de sangre seca flota en la roca el esqueleto de fuera

pez anzuelo del pez redondo hueco

cosido con alambres azules a una boca de trapo

a través de la piel absorbe el agua a través de la piel expulsa el agua

fósil sin párpados ni nombre flota a la deriva ardiente y ocre

radiografía del pez en las alturas su radiante espuma

rupestre cuando las cuevas estaban todavía llenas de un agua inmóvil

la espina oculta entre las comisuras de la risa

fosforesce en la piedra envuelta en vaho

denso verde vaho en cada hueco suyo de carne o agua cruda

hace un nido de saliva en la pared de enfrente

lítico pez punzón pez hacha pez cuchillo del pez que corta el agua

pez de vidrio volcánico en los albores de la animalidad

oscuro imán en el hueco craneal extinto pez sin lengua

supraceleste desnudo inamovible fusiforme esférico cilíndrico rojo

quien distingue entre las aguas pluviales y las aguas residuales

las aletas dorsales atrofiadas en el juego de los peces cruzados

columna y agujero

indistinto entre la multitud de ceros a la izquierda del erizo negro

oye por el cráneo a través del yeso la pared de adentro

entre las piedras llenas de animales pintados que nada ilumina

pez afuera del pez cuando ya su esqueleto no es su jaula

la saliva dorada y la música oculta

quien no distingue la pudrición del suelo de los nuevos tallos de la cola

pez colgante

por un sesgo imprevisto regresa al agua amarga debajo de la lengua

la líquida tortura de la sal en los abismos que ilumina

pez anzuelo del pez redondo hueso

espina de la luna atravesada en la garganta

el esqueleto interno disolviéndose en el azogue de su espejo

sol verde fosforece entre las aguas negras

fosa del pez sediento que otro pez imagina en su desierto

Vertical Fish / *grafitti*

traced with a finger on the salty surface of a wall
with a bladder of dry blood it floats in rock its skeleton outside it
fish fish hook round hole
its feather-duster mouth stitched with blue wires
through skin water sucks in through skin water is expelled
lidless nameless fossil adrift hot and ocher
X-ray of the fish at its peak its radiant spume
mineralized when caves were still filled with tranquil water
the thorn hidden in the corners of phosphorescent
laugh caught in the mist-wrapped rock
a dense green mist in each pocket of flesh or primal water
forms a nest of saliva on the facing wall
lytic fish hatchetfish awl fish fish knifing through water
volcanic glass fish in the dawn of animality
dark magnetism in the cranial hollow extinct fish before language
cerulean naked fixed spherical spindle-shaped cylindrical red
discerning stormwater from wastewater
dorsal fins atrophied in the genetic play of crossbreeding fish
column and hole
indistinguishable from crowded zeros to the left of black sea urchins
it hears through the plaster to the interior wall
between stones chock-full with painted animals that nothing illuminates
fish emerging from fish through the unlocked skeleton
golden saliva and fugitive music
senseless to freshly putrefying tail-stems on the ground
hanging fish
unimaginably distorted turned to bitter water under the tongue
the salt-tortured liquid in abysses that illumine
fish fish hook round hole
the moon's thorn piercing its throat
its internal skeleton dissolving in the quicksilver of a mirror
a green sun phosphorescing under black water
fossa of the thirsting fish imagined by another fish in its desert

hileras de espinas irisadas bajo las estrellas
bajo el lodo del tiempo pez come pez es la verdad más honda
las escamas violetas en las profundidades de la tierra
vidrio molido la sal rojiza relumbra entre su piel
la hembra con la aleta caudal en media luna desova el primer huevo
pez uña el tragaluz desdobla
a través de la piel absorbe el agua a través de la piel expulsa el agua
grito del pez babeante mortificado en su lecho de hojas
canta en silencio como un ramo de sal en la cabeza

rows of iridescent thorns below the stars
below the mud of time fish eating fish the surest verity
violet scales throughout all the earth's layers
salt like ground glass red-glowing from dead scales
the female whose caudal fin stiffens as she spawns the first egg
fingernail fish the skylight opened
through skin water sucks in through skin water is expelled
scream of a fish drooling mortified in its leafy bed
in silence it sings in silence like a bouquet of salt in the mind

13

Pienso mientras camino
en estas dos visiones contrapuestas
pero que en realidad se compenetran:
el abismo carnal en el que desemboca cada cosa
y esta aguda visión de los hilos de aire
que todo lo penetran y conectan

Me detengo y levanto una piedra
y este gesto que he realizado infinidad de veces
no sólo en mí sino en cuantos fueron antes de mí
y en los que serán
este gesto de detenerme a medio paso
a levantar una piedra
la misma y otra cada vez
me conmueve más allá de mí mismo
y al mirar en mis dedos
los hilos (violetas) que en ella se concretan
y *la forma que tiene*
mis ojos se entrecierran fijamente
y descubro
en *su peso maravilloso* en el hueco de mi mano
en su lívido color de piel insomne
y en las venas sólo por un momento
entrevistas que la cruzan

y que prolongan los hilos de mis manos
y desembocan en este lago de aire iluminado
que no sólo la tarde y la carne están en ella contenidas y
como condensadas confundidas
sino también *la idea*
que de ellas—entre los dedos—
me he formado

13

As I walk I'm holding in mind
two visions in counterpoint
or better yet two co-penetrating visions:
the carnal abyss where all empties out
and my vivid perception of airborne threads
that interweave and connect everything

I pause to pick up a stone
and this act which I've repeated countless times
not only as myself but as how many before me
and how many afterward
this gesture of half stopping
to pick up a stone
an act singular and similar at once
moves me beyond myself
so that when I look at my fingers
at the (violet) filaments that congregate in the stone
and at the form it takes
I squint fixedly
and find
in this *marvelous density* in the hollow of my hand
in its livid insomniac paleness
and in its veins dialogues
that only for a moment
crisscross

joining the filaments in my hands
and emptying out into the lake of luminous air
where not only this afternoon but the flesh is contained
in knotted confusions
and I also find—between my fingers—
that idea from which
I myself have taken shape

No puedo conservarla me digo
esta piedra no puedo conservarla
me quemaría las manos si volviera a tocarla
me sacaría los ojos si intentara mirar…
Y al aire sin pensar la lanzo

                      y luego me arrepiento

cuando miro su arco
de carne iluminada en el aire suspenso
antes de ir a perderse
—miembro eterno una vez más perdido—
en la mental profundidad del lago
la elemental profundidad del agua
en su caída
hasta el fondo de sí misma

Y sigo caminando…

I tell myself I can't keep
the stone can't keep it
it would burn me if I handled it any longer
it would bruise my eyes if I stared…
And so I fling it into the air

                           and immediately regret it

when I see the arc
of flesh luminous in the suspended sky
before finally it disappears
—steady companion lost again—
in the mental depths of the lake
the elemental depths of the water
in its fall
to the bottom of itself

As I go on walking…

Esporas

(a)

Lo interminable verde • Planas de plantas • Caligrafía raigal

Maraña escrita • Verbo tallo • Decir salvia

Estilo de las flores • Estigma de la lengua • Venas de la hoja

Palabra-enzima • Vaina-letra • Caña-sílaba

Verso labiado • Verso irídeo • Verso deshiscente

Verso móreo • Verso silvestre • Verso rusco

Ritmo y lino • Lirio y ripio • Rama y rima

Rima talar • Rima sésil • Margen foliar

Bulbo ideográfico • Cáñamo currente • Línea inflorescente

Nuez del pensamiento • Membrana sonora • Raíz lingual

Spores

(a)

Interminable verdancy • Plains of plants • Calligraphic raceme

Written tangle • Verb stem • Speaking spearmint

Style of flowers • Tongue's stigma • Veins of leaves

Word-enzyme • Letter-husk • Syllable-stylus

Labiate verse • Iridious verse • Dehiscent verse

Nut-brown verse • Wild verse • Butcher's broom verse

Rhythm and rubble • Lily and line • Bough and ballad

Felled rhyme • Sessile rhyme • Foliate margin

Ideographic bulb • Hemp undertow • Inflorescent line

Thought's nut • Sonorous membrane • Lingual root

(b)

Estro y siniestro   •   Flora y fabla   •   Alalia y aloba

Himnos frutales   •   Racimos de rimas   •   Higos verbales

Hierba lira   •   Bosque es tinta   •   Voz que espina

Hablar lígulas   •   Balbucir bulbos   •   Secretear setas

Musitar musgos   •   Haz de signos   •   Gritar palmas

Escandir polen   •   Sembrar erratas   •   Violar tinta

Salvia verba   •   Hongo eco   •   Labia ova

Caña silva   •   Décima espina   •   Fronda y oda

Cardo salmo   •   Piracanto   •   Helecho criptogramático

Grama y grafía   •   Cifrar esporas   •   Descifrar fibras

(b)

Inspiration and expiration • Flora and fable • Alalia and aloba

Fruitful hymns • Racemes of rhymes • Verbal figs

Herb lyre • Forest as ink • Thorny voice

Speaking in ligules • Babbling bulbs • Shushing mushrooms

Mumbling mosses • Shaft of signs • Shouting palms

Scanning pollen • Planting misprints • Ravishing ink

Verbal sap • Echoing fungus • Lettuce lips

Forest stylus • Decasyllabic salvia • Frond and ode

Thistle psalm • Pyrocanthus • Cryptographic bracken

Grass and grapheme • Encrypting spores • Deciphering fibers

Digitaria exilis

I

Como vuelve de pronto / un viejo sueño
vi la estrella salvaje / cruzar los cielos

Pájaro espantapájaros / sombras desnuda
en rincones hirsutos / su luz azula

Filos inesperados / franjas oblicuas
tejen la red verdosa / de las ortigas

Tan diminutos granos / los más pequeños
guardan entre los dedos / un universo

Frágiles estructuras / iluminadas
una esfera invisible / me señalaban

2

Cuando llega la lluvia / se borra el cielo
la saliva brillante / del perro negro

Tras la cara del pájaro / desafinado
vi una esfera más clara / del otro lado

Oculta esfera hueca / la más liviana
insospechada a medias / elucidaba

La semilla de vidrio / la noche inquieta
la nostalgia de Sirio / bajo la lengua

Y el astro de diamante / que nadie ha visto
flotaba en mi cabeza / grano de mijo

Digitaria exilis

1

It comes from nowhere / that old dream
of seeing the wild dogstar / cross the sky

Crow scarecrow / naked shadows
in bristling furrows / the light goes blue

Startling needlepoints / angled stripes
weave a greeny net / of nettles

Such minuscule / and durant seeds
stand guard in fingering leaves / over a universe

A fragile configuration / lit up
an invisible sphere of light / signaling

2

When rain comes / the sky smudges out
bright spittle / of a black dog

Beyond the tuneless / crow's face
I make out a clearer sphere / parallactic

A recessive hidden sphere / barely there
unsuspected half / enlightening

The crystalline seed / disquiets the night
a nostalgia for Sirius / under my tongue

And the diamond star / no one has yet seen
floating through my mind / a grain of millet

Part II

Zagreo

El corazón sagrado de Zagreo
rodaba entre cenizas por el suelo

Espejo entre juguetes elegido
juguete de los perros sin el niño

Al acecho palpita entre las piedras
el reflejo sangrante de la hiedra

Casi invisible si su luz no fuera
leve zumbo de vida a ras de tierra

Zagreus

The sacred heart Zagreus bore
rolled in ash across the floor

A mirror picks between two toys
the toy of dogs who had no boy

Behind the rocks, pulsant, hiding,
bloody reflections, creeping ivy

Invisible but for its own light
the faint ground-level hum of life

Una linfa dorada lo alimenta
en la luz que destila se deleita

Irradian de su cuerpo repartido
los miembros que se agitan tras el vidrio

Imagen del espejo enrarecido
la blanca faz del cazador furtivo

Enredo de rebrillos ominosos
el reflejo que encarna entre los ojos

Golden lymph provides the measured
light that parcels out this pleasure

His comely trunk might seem to pass
into limbs that gesture at the glass

An image catching in the mirror:
pallid face, the furtive hunter

Trapped in glower, reflections rise;
incarnations between his eyes

Incapaces de ver entre hebras rotas
el hilo fino que cruza las cosas

Irradia en la penumbra del eclipse
el rastro inocultable de oro y tizne

Luz que la luz del vidrio apenas rosa
la repentina mano de una diosa

Lo alza en el aire al aire y se lo lleva
y de la tierra un haz añil se eleva

In strands that flare in all directions
you lose the one thread of connection

Through the penumbra of eclipse
a radiant track of grime and glitz

The mirror shows a quick pink band
of light or god's shapeliest hand

From air to air he's carried down
a blue shaft rises from the ground

Late en sus dedos la encarnada huella
del imantado astro la entretela

Más pensada que vista luz oculta
la solícita mano que lo ausculta

Y al tocarlo lo escucha y lo piensa
y al pensar lo descubre y lo tienta

Salta el nudo al contacto del filo
¡Si sigue en vilo el corazón del niño!

Your fingers find the incarnate trace
of the magnetic star they interlace

Dark light far more felt than stated
probed by hand and auscultated

And at your touch, it listens, thinks
and thinking, sees itself and blinks

You pass the nub to reach the start
Afloat in air, your child's heart!

Como un cristal ardiente blanco enjambre
que al rezumar la luz en luz se parte

Al suelo cae la cal que lo cubría
vidrio desnudo transparenta el día

El día que nace dentro del dios mismo
y se prolonga en los hilos del vidrio

Y aletea la víscera sublime
se desbordan sus vasos irascibles

A hive of glowing white-hot glass
leaks light until its light has passed

A spilled whitewash that couldn't stay
the naked see-through glass of day

From this same god the day comes clear
and pulses through threads of mirror

Sublime the viscera's muted flapping
its flooded vessels overlapping

Y de pronto se tiñen en el aire
del oro las violetas de la tarde

Se deshila la luz en los zarcillos
y el vidrio se desangra por sus brillos

El círculo sanguíneo del espejo
o el reflejo que encarna en el reflejo

Y de pronto otra mano lo levanta
hasta el oscuro hueco de una estatua

La frente se ilumina y se despierta
el corazón deseante de la hiedra
y zumba cada vena y cada hebra

And then the golden air, it blooms
with sudden violets, afternoon

As light undoes itself and peens
it seems the glass bleeds in the sheen

A blood disc in the mirror or
the incarnate image coming clearer

You raise your other hand into
the hidden hole of the statue

Your mind lights up with a start
there in the ivy's lascivious heart
each vein buzzing in every part

Part III

Escrito en un grano de sal

A la luz mental de las estrellas
Halos / sal / hados
Leer la sal
Agua y piedra / la primera tierra
La sal de la saliva
Honda alba habita mi cráneo / a contraluz incandescente labio
Cielo y sal / nada más
Sal Eros

Montes blancos / en la mano
La mosca come sal
En cada cara / refleja / otro cielo / reflejado
Adarce de la luz entre las hojas
Geométricas construcciones / de un agua mental
Fractura de flor inversa / la sal se quiebra / se quiebra / la sal pétrea
Mineral oculto / incoloro y puro
Simple mente sal

Ah las maravillosas distancias de lo mínimo
Umbrátil emerge / lúcida invisible / sal intransparente / sílice

Oculta en su blancura / como la estrella inscrita en cada grano
Reflejante / reflejada / reflejaba… el agua
Y en los labios... rastros

Written in a Grain of Salt

In the mindful light of the stars
Halite / salt / fate
Reading the salt
Water and stone / the first earth
Saliva's salt
Fathomless dawn alive in my skull / lips backlit with incandescence
Air and salt / nothing else
Salt Eros

White mountains / at hand
A fly licking the salt
Each face / reflects / another sky / reflected
Adarce of light in the leaves
Geometric constructions / of the mind's water
Fractures in salt flowers / reversed in fissures / fissures / in fossilizing salt
Cryptic minerals / colorless and pure
Elemental mind salt

Ah the marvelous distances of the umbratile
Minimum emerge / as lucid invisible / untranslucent salt / silica

Encrypted in its white script / as the star in each grain
Reflective / reflectant / reflected… water
And on my lips… its traces

(green fluorite)

El contacto
entre la ínfima irradiación
color cobalto
de las huellas de mis dedos
y la intensa
irradiación naranja
de este trozo opaco
de fluorita verde
que sostengo entre los dedos
anticipa
—al más simple nivel
de la irradiante luminiscencia
de los cuerpos distantes
y esplendentes—
el inminente encuentro
de mi epidermis y el cristal
y el más profundo acercamiento
entre planos internos
que se funden
—vibraciones de la luz
convertidas en música—
entre el calor mineral que me transmite
y las cristalinas imágenes
que se van
construyendo tras mis ojos

Idénticos
durante un instante incierto
en que el interior del cúbico cristal
y mi cabeza cuadrada
parecen alojar
en el apacible flujo
de sus líneas rectas
y sus ángulos equívocos

(green fluorite)

The contact
between the feeble cobalt-
colored radiation
of my fingerprints
and the intense
orange radiation
of this opaque piece
of green fluorite
I hold between fingers
gives rise
—at the simplest level
of the radiant glow
of these distant and
splendid bodies—
to the imminent encounter
of my skin and the crystal
and the deepest rapprochement
between inner planes
that fuse
—vibrations of light
converted to music—
between the mineral heat that transports me
and the crystalline images
locking into place
behind my eyes

Identical
for a quivering moment
in which the interior of the cubic crystal
and my squarish head
seem to accommodate—
in the fluid flow
of straight lines
and their misleading angles—

una misma figura translucente
que los hilos de la luz
llevan y traen
desde el ácuo interior de la piedra
y su convulsa red vacía
hasta un lugar
sin espacio
que de pronto
entre mis dedos
se abre

Hoy al fin vista
a la luz de otro día
en secreta
consonancia
con las formas que no muestra
y en todo el maravillante portento
de su disonante
transparencia
como a través del ojo
de una cerradura de cristal
que permitiera al ojo
acostumbrado a la cambiante
perspectiva
de las sombras sin rostro
fijar
en el vaivén de las visiones contrapuestas
la infinitesimal inclusión
de la última imagen imperecedera
y cierta

Un cuerpo azul
desnudo a simple vista
—ese anhelo sin fin
del tacto que incandece en el centro
sin centro

an identical translucent figure
that threads of light
take and bring
from the aqueous interior of the stone
and its convulsively vibrating net
to some spaceless
place
between my fingers
which instantly
clicks open

Seen again now
in the light of another day
in secret
consonance
with its hidden patterns
and in all the portentous marvel
of its dissonant
transparency
as though glimpsed through the eye
of a crystalline lock
that permits the eye
accustomed to the changing
perspective
of the faceless shadows
to determine
in the vacillation of opposing views
the infinitesimal designation
of the last and most
enduring image

A naked blue
body in plain sight
—that endless longing
for touch incandescing at the centerless
center

de cada pensamiento—
se yergue
mutilado y lascivo
entre lazos de sombra que no cesan
de moverse
—muñones violáceos
de piernas y brazos—
y sólo es visible
bajo la oblicua luz que lo cruza
y desdobla
entre mis dedos
su figura
al tiempo que me aclara y me contiene
y en un deslumbramiento
cifra
el instante en que lo veo
y la incolora claridad del cuarto

of every thought—
it stands
maimed and lascivious
between coiled shadows that never stop
moving
—violet stumps
of legs and arms—
and it's only visible
under the oblique light which flickers across it
its form unfolding
between my fingers
while it declares me and contains me
and in its dazzle
encodes
the instant in which I see it
and the colorless clarity of this room

Acanto

a / red

Disimula su belleza
con gesto de indiferencia
y su complicada sombra
en el agua se refleja

Bajo un tejido tan puro
hecho de hilos transparentes
siente la piedra el impulso
de reflejarse en la fuente

Y la sombra que proyecta
en el agua se confunde
y se hace tan blanca y simple
que en el agua se diluye

Luz oscura y descarnada
desvela la superficie
el agua turbia transluce
y deja ver sus raíces

Hondos finos hilos negros
que se enredan en el agua
fija red de los cabellos
en que se envuelve la estatua

La transparente estructura
donde se cierne su sombra
refracta en el agua oscura
la claridad que despoja

Sombra de imagen ausente
en tenue urdimbre de venas
tiñe el agua de la fuente
y desde abajo hace señas

Acanthus

a / net

It dissembles its loveliness
with an air of indifference
and its complicated shadow
reflects in the water

Under so pure a tissue
of transparent threads
the rock registers a pulse
projected from the source

And the shadow projected
across water blends
and goes so white and lucid
that it dilutes itself in the water

The dark and fleshless light
unveils the surface
a turbid water transluces
and bares its roots

Sheer depths black threads
snared in the water
a fixed hairnet
wrapped around the statue

The transparent structure
with its hovering shadow
is refracted in dark water
spoiling its clarity

The shadow of a missing image
in a tenuous warp of veins
stains the water at its source
and from below beckons

Sinsabor del acitrón

Se trasluce el sol...

Como si no acabara de masticarlo nunca / como si no supiera que ya no sabe
a nada / como a través de un vidrio / desde la otra mañana / aquella calle sola
/ desde un invierno intacto / otra mañana helada

Vidrio vivo por dentro / en su red de reflejos / entre aristas que asoman de
infantiles resabios / sol que no sale aún / pero que ya ilumina la corteza a trasluz
/ una sombra insipiente o una duda jocosa / me cruzó por los ojos y me tocó
los labios

De aquella fruta opaca / la translúcida pulpa / por dentro iluminaba / lo que
aún no sabía / el vidriado espejismo / apenas alcanzado / la dulzura del ámbar
/ que mi vista anegaba / y esta red que mi lengua fue dejando vacía

Y aun su luz acre guarda / un ácido secreto / o un resplandor errante / que de
pronto restalla

Y la sombra furtiva / como un deslumbramiento / daba vuelta a la esquina
como a través de un sueño / en el instante mismo en que el filo del sol y la costra
de azúcar se fundían en mi boca / y el cercano horizonte / me cortaba el aliento

Como si no supiera / que a cada dentellada / la calle centellea / y el paladar se
empapa / como si no alcanzara / a saber todavía / desde el áspero hueco que
mis dientes traspasan / que el insípido oro de la luz que regresa / es la sombra
que escapa

Perspectivas cambiantes / entrecruzan reflejos / sobre una misma cara que
miro a la distancia / como a través de un vidrio / por atrás de mis ojos / a la
luz que se fuga / ilusión del recuerdo / y en los ojos del niño / otra sonrisa
alumbra

Citron's Bitterness

The sun transluces...

As if I couldn't stop chewing it / as if I didn't know nothing is known / as through a window / onto another morning / this single street / through a winter intact / another icy dawn

Life passes through glass / through its net of reflections / along sharp edges that loom from the aftertastes of childhood / sun still not out / but the bark going lucent already in the near-light / an incipient shadow or a ludic doubt / flitting across my eyes and grazing my lips

From that cloudy fruit / the translucent pulp / lit within / what couldn't have been known / the glazed mirage / almost within reach / a sweetness of amber / flooding my eyes / and this net emptied of my language

And yet even its light has a sour / bite a masked acidity / or a snap / of errant blaze

And the furtive shadow / a kind of bewilderment / turned the corner as in a dream / at the same moment the sun's spike and crusted sugar melted in my mouth / and the near horizon / cut off my breath

As if I didn't know / that with each bite / the street flashed / and my palate was besieged / as if I wouldn't ever / come to realize / from the astringent hollow my teeth tore through / that this insipid golden returning light is / escaping shadow

Shifting perspectives / crosshatch my ruminations / on the same face
I make out in the distance / as through a glass / from behind my eyes / to light that spills out / an illusion of memory / and my child's eyes / are beaming

Entre las fibras finas / que no saben a nada / sino a la pura miel de este vidrio insondable / ah dulce lucidez / que a mi gusto revela / un segundo espejismo de esa misma mañana / de un invierno radiante

En tu espejo sin brillo / regresa aquel vislumbre / que alguna vez tuviera / la sombra que refleja y mis secretos urde / cuando roza mis labios / y un resplandor incierto / que no termina nunca / cristaliza en azúcar el corazón del cactus

Y siento otra dulzura debajo de la lengua / como un dejo terroso en las venas doradas / que colma mis sentidos y despierta mi anhelo / como fulge en el vidrio la cruda resolana / de tocar bajo tierra / disuelta en mi saliva / amarilla y opaca / la raíz del destello

Between fine fibers / that know nothing / but the pure honey of this unfathomable glass / ah sweet lucidity / which reveals to my taste / a second mirage of that same morning / in a radiant winter

In your lusterless mirror / the shimmer you once had / returns / the shadow demonstrating and plaiting my secrets / when it brushes my lips / and an uncertain radiance / that never ends / crystallizes as sugar in the heart of a cactus

And I sense another sweetness under my tongue / like dross leftover in mined veins / that floods me with feeling and spikes my need / like a glint in the glass the raw and promising / joining underground / dissolve in my saliva / thick and yellow / the scintillant root

El résped de su verbo

Trastoca trasnombra
translúcida línea
la víbora el verbo
traslapa su sombra

Obseso tatuaje
hileras de manchas
trasuda la estrella
lenguaje de escamas

Trasmina trashoja
miríadas de horas
traslada trastumba
traspasa la hoja

Desliza en el suelo
su transversa vara
que se transfigura
en otra palabra

Su doble escritura
de piel y su rastro
transcribe en la arena
la ruta de un astro

Trasunto de linfa
transluce en el vaso
transfunde otra tinta
la luz del ocaso

Arena o saliva
transpone las letras
y entre las espinas
despliega su tela

Its Verb's Forked Tongue

Transforms transnominates
translucent line
the viper the verb
translades its shadow

Tattoo freak
from rows of spots
a star transudes
a language of scales

Transposes transleafs
myriads of hours
transmigrates transtombs
transversing the leaf

As it glides the floor
its transverse wand
transforms it
into an other word

Its double writing
of skin and track
transcribed in sand
a star's path

The lymph transcript
transluces behind glass
other inks
transfusing twilight

Sand or saliva
transposes the letters
and over the points
casts its web

Translúcida escama
es cada palabra
en su movimiento
que no dice nada

Móvil escritura
de fuerzas y esferas
que alterna y transmuta
en granos de arena

Trasueña su sueño
trasnuda su silbo
siempre vinculada
al Verso divino
y al precioso Signo

Each word a trans-
lucent scale
moving along
saying nothing

Mobile script
of fields and forces
that shift and transmute
over grains of sand

The transdreaming dream
transnatures its hiss
inseverable from
divine Verse
and the decisive Sign

[Nudo]

(d)

Entre [tocar] la imagen y [tocar] la serpiente
lo que vive [en] cada uno de los pedazos
de la [noche]
que recomienza

Entre el despertar [de] la piedra y los cristales
del labro
la sangre [sube]

Entre [trocar] imago por imagen
sin margen [para] el ojo
el [olor] que despide [su] sombra
al ampararse

Entre [entrar] a una imagen y [pal-]
parla
en la vitrina un áspid que declina
entre flores de azúcar que lenta [disuelve]
la orilla

Entre la v de labios [de] la víbora
y el cadáver adentro
[silba] viendo

Entre la muda [transparencia] de su muda
y el silencio [de] muerte de su forma

Entrever [y] mirar
opaca [o] vista
la [forma] que [se] enrolla [entre] las formas
la [visión] invisible
[debajo] de la costra

[Knot]

(d)

Between [touching] the image and [touching] the snake
living [in] each of the pieces
of the [night]
starting up again

Between the wakening [of] stone and labrum
crystals
blood [rises]

Between [exchanging] imago for image
with no margins [for] the eye
the [scent] discharging [its] shadow
for shelter

Between [entering] an image and [be-]
speaking it
an asp settles in the window box
between sugar-flowers slowly [dissolving]
the border

Between the v of the lips [of] the snake
and the corpse inside
seeing [sibilates]

Between its molting's mute [transparency]
and the lethal silence [of] its form

Glimpsing [and] taking in
dull [or] vivid
the [form] that coils [on] itself [among] forms
the [vision] invisible
[under] the scurf

Y la imagen al fondo de la imagen
[translúcida] en otra [imagen] se transluce

> *Entre holanes amarillos*
> *ocultaba los colmillos...*

And the image in the depths of the image
[translucent] in another [image] translucing

Between yellow frets
the concealed fangs...

A Note on the Translation

This translation was spurred into a gallop by Sheila Lanham through her US Poets in Mexico program. I had translated some of Alfonso's poems and he had translated and published some of mine in the early 1990s, soon after we met and realized how much we had in common, not only our passion for rocks, plants, reptiles, and butoh, but also our approach to innovative poetics.

Sheila offered us a two-week residency in Mexico. We spent one week with a film crew in Xalapa, visiting the Clavijero Botanical Gardens, Macuiltepetl Park on top of the Xalapa volcano, the Cerro de las Culebras, and the extensive Xico waterfalls. The next week we holed up in a hotel and worked through the versions of translations that we had drafted several months earlier.

Both of us are grateful to Sheila and the US Poets in Mexico program for the opportunity to devote ourselves to this project.

About the Translator

Forrest Gander was born in the Mojave Desert and grew up in Virginia. He is a writer and translator with degrees in geology and English literature. Among his recent books are *Eiko & Koma* and two anthologies: *Panic Cure: Poetry from Spain for the 21st Century* and *Pinholes in the Night: Essential Poems from Latin America* (with Raúl Zurita). Gander's book *Core Samples from the World,* an investigation into the way the self is revised and translated in encounters with the foreign, was a finalist for the Pulitzer Prize and the National Book Critics Circle Award. He is the Adele Kellenberg Seaver Professor of Literary Arts and Comparative Literature at Brown University.

Poetry is vital to language and living. Since 1972, Copper Canyon Press has published extraordinary poetry from around the world to engage the imaginations and intellects of readers, writers, booksellers, librarians, teachers, students, and donors.

This publication was made possible through the support of the Program for Translation (PROTRAD) funded by the national cultural institutions of Mexico.

WE ARE GRATEFUL FOR THE MAJOR SUPPORT PROVIDED BY:

THE PAUL G. ALLEN
FAMILY FOUNDATION

THE MAURER FAMILY
FOUNDATION

NATIONAL
ENDOWMENT
FOR THE ARTS

WASHINGTON STATE
ARTS COMMISSION

Anonymous
Arcadia Fund
John Branch
Diana and Jay Broze
Beroz Ferrell & The Point, llc
Janet and Les Cox
Mimi Gardner Gates
Gull Industries, Inc.
on behalf of William and Ruth True
Mark Hamilton and Suzie Rapp
Carolyn and Robert Hedin
Steven Myron Holl
Lakeside Industries, Inc.
on behalf of Jeanne Marie Lee
Maureen Lee and Mark Busto
Brice Marden
New Mexico Community Foundation
H. Stewart Parker
Penny and Jerry Peabody
Joseph C. Roberts
Cynthia Lovelace Sears and Frank Buxton
The Seattle Foundation
Dan Waggoner
Charles and Barbara Wright
The dedicated interns and faithful
volunteers of Copper Canyon Press

To learn more about underwriting Copper Canyon Press titles,
please call 360-385-4925 ext. 103

The Chinese character for poetry is made up of two parts:
"word" and "temple." It also serves as pressmark for
Copper Canyon Press.

The poems are set in Adobe Garamond, with titles set in Whitney.
Book design and composition by Phil Kovacevich.